P9-DYY-405

The Poet's Song: Poetry from a troubled youth

Poetae Publishing

Philadelphia, Pa 19139

Contact: (267) 777-8286

To the center
"2015"

Matthew Williams

Foreword

He calls it plugging in. He ties his afro into a bun, swings his book bag across one shoulder and steps outside. He puts his headphones in, turns the music off and walks. If you see him you would think he is listening to music but he's not. It's his escape. He used to walk around, his head held high, smiling, and then the world found him. Quick conversations, judgmental stares, crooked smiles, he was losing himself. He started being ashamed of his body and self-conscious of his hair, so much so that he tried to cover it, hide it. He would wear black socks everyday so nobody would notice the holes in his favorite pair of black shoes. His native language of "wats good bull" got forgotten. He rather go silent than be made fun of for how he spoke. He started walking quickly, eyes down on the ground hoping nobody would notice him. Hoping that he would just fit in. He used to be full of wonder, imagination and curiosity. He used to live, but now he's just alive. I'm just alive.

Growing up, I can remember people telling me that I would never amount to anything. For most of adolescence, I let their perceptions become my realities and I held back. I stopped pursuing my art and in many ways tried to suppress it. I wasn't necessarily a bad kid, but I can remember moments of just feeling raw anger – anger that was mainly directed at my family and friends for not understanding, or choosing not to understand, my struggle.

A lot of this internal struggle came from growing up without a father, being a part of a family that were not entirely my biological family, and having several who on a daily basis reminded me of that fact, not having siblings close to me in age, and the list goes on. This is not to say my family didn't care or love me, but rather to highlight the emotional struggle I was dealing with during adolescence. Throughout my childhood, I was surrounded by drugs, violence, poverty, sickness and fear. This was my normal – my reality. I assumed everyone else lived this way too. I was wrong. This was my life growing up in the inner city, where things that became my normal really wasn't everyone else's normal.

Then one day I found poetry in the third grade and it changed my life. My first poem I had ever written was called "Why":

Why are you outside with those thugs selling drugs?

Why aren't you in the house teaching your daughter to read some math or giving your two year old son a bath?

Why are you chewing on a piece of hay instead of cooking with your wife all day?

Why are you smoking with those boys instead of telling your daughter about them? That they steal and kill just for a thrill.

Why just why

And with my first poem, a change in my life began to happen. I didn't learn how to write poetry in some fancy school or private institute; my learning came one night from watching a poet slamming on T.V. I heard his passion, the intensity in his voice and I heard his story. It was my story. I picked up my pen and have not been able to put it down since. There were times when I had people criticize my poetry. I had somebody rip my poetry in half in front of me while telling me I would never amount to anything. I remember being encouraged to do more "practical things" and to follow more "realistic" careers. Luckily, though, there was another group of people whispering in my ear, telling me that I could *do* anything and *be* anything my heart desired, especially if my faith in Christ was strong. And so, because of these supporters and my personal spiritual convictions, the sky became limitless once more and the journey of telling my story began.

The collection of poetry that follows are my stories: a young boy yearning for a father, a teen grappling with death and sexuality, a college student struggling to find his place and purpose in life. Many of the stories will talk about the most vulnerable times in my life; others will just be whimsical poems with no meaning whatsoever. I share these stories not for myself, but for the next generation of dreamers who are labeled "troubled" or "different". For the next generation of dreamers who are being told you can't and won't succeed. For the next generation of dreamers who are on the verge of giving up. I want this collection of poems to serve as a message that anything is possible if you try, and even if you fail, then at least you tried. After many years of pain, struggle, and hurt, I have learned that nothing beats failure except effort and whether one fails or succeeds comes down to his trying. This, then, is my try, my effort, my attempt.

He has made his move. He has finally unplugged. He has taken the leap and spread his wings. Let's watch him fly.

~The Shy Poet

Thanks and Dedication

I would like to thank everybody who was with me through this long journey. My countless number of friends who have read every single poem I have ever written, both good and bad. I would like to thank my family for their love and support, especially when times got rough. I would like to also thank the people who really motivated me to get my book published, my mother and sister, the Dennis family, Travis Smith, Jazmine Renee, Jojo Pope, Zaire Best, Susan Delp, countless teachers, family, friends and everybody in-between.

I like to give thanks and praise to God, without whom this book would not be possible.

This book is dedicated to two generations in my life. The generations who have come before me and have gone, Ruth Evans, Mildred Edwards, Gwen Edwards, and Kevin Edwards.

But also to the generation coming after me,

Cianni, Enya, Kaylin, Myleena , Kiera, Brandon, Bryce, Christian, Amir, Quadir, Jonathan and many many others. The future is yours for the taking.

Table of Contents

I am here

Give me a chance

And watch me rise

Victorious, soaring under my own strength.

Invite me to your table, into your heart, love me, listen to my story but…

NEVER try and silence me for it will be in vain cause I'll always rise.

~This poem is dedicated to the graduating class of Beatrice Rafferty Elementary School 2014.

Keep strong and speak with conviction even when others try and silence you.

Keep moving forward and know I'm proud of ya'll~

Let's talk....

"It's okay if you graduate college with all C's. We all know it's really hard for students in your situation." I remember those words as if they were spoken yesterday. They came from an administrator on my second day of college orientation and were meant to make me feel welcomed. To them I was just a poor black kid from the ghetto who spoke slang and would only perform mediocre at their prestigious "liberal" university. My situation in reality was that I was a poor black kid from the ghetto who spoke slang, who worked his ass off for four years to get into their prestigious "liberal" university, and who was hungry for success. A week later I wrote my first paper in college and received an F with a note attached saying "this is terrible and not college material. I'm not sure how you got here. I'll be emailing your deans". Sure enough, with that one F, I had let their misguided assumptions about me come true, at least that is how I felt.

Approximately one month later, I then learned it is better to get a B in class than to raise my hand and have people laugh and snicker at me when I occasionally used a slang word. After just one semester I was burnt out, tired of constantly changing how I spoke in class, dressed, wrote, and ate. By that point, all I really wanted was a piece of home – my momma's homemade sweet tea, deep fried country style chicken and my comfortable bed. I went home after that first semester a different person. I went into college with a perfect 4.0 GPA, second in my class, first generation college student, and one, I might add, who never received a grade lower than an A-. However, I came out of that first semester with a different set of credentials: a victim of racism, a student with his first F, and young man who, for the first time in his life, was ashamed of his lack of privilege and identity. I felt like I was at a fork in the road – do I return and suffer more of the same fate, or apply to a college where I knew I would feel more "at home"? My family had always told me to attend an HBCU, historically black college and university, and for the first time, I began to think they were right.

One week before I was to return to college, my uncle and I spent time talking about all the things I had been experiencing. At the end of the conversation, he simply sat back, let out a sigh and said, "That's a lot." He then leaned forward and said, "God only tests those he wants to use in life and he is going to use you. Nobody finishes college in a day. I don't care if it takes you three years or ten, I know you will finish. You can do all things in Christ who strengthens you. He loves you, your grandmother loves you and I love you. Nobody can tell you who you are, only you can, so *tell them who you are*. Put on the armor of God and be proud of everything you have and don't have because I'm proud of you. You are becoming a good man and I love you".

There wasn't a day that went by during my second semester that I didn't think about those words. In fact, it was those words that refueled my hunger once more. I would achieve everything I had set out to do: prove everyone who had ever doubted me wrong, support my family so they didn't have to struggle anymore, give my mom back everything she gave me growing up, provide for my sister, nieces, my future family, and share my story with my community and the world. My reality is that I am a poor black boy from the hood who speaks slang. I don't have the most expensive clothes. Yes I fail, but I learn from my mistakes so that I can get back on the bull and ride it into the sunset. Today as I write this I am a junior in college, and I am motivated now more than ever before. My grades are up, my GPA is solid, I am stepping into my blessing and I am proud of every aspect of my life – the good, bad, poor, rich, ugly…. I know that I can do all things through Christ and that my strength cometh from him. At the end of the day, it's not about how long you stay down once you have fallen; it's about making sure you *do* get back up.

The Shadows That Dance Forever

In the light of the moon two shadows dance.
Forever and ever the two will be,
like the burning stars in the midnight sky,
together even when their shadows fade.

Let their fire burn under the calm sea,
defying all odds placed upon their heads,
as the seas rage and crash all night because,
forever and ever the two will be.

When the heavens open and pour sweet rain,
to distract the lovers from their melodies,
the shadows grow stronger and dance all night,
together even when their shadows fade.

Sweet dreamers dream and dancers dance with glee.
May their voices be heard with quiet words,
like shadows drowning from love lost, but still,
forever and ever the two will be.

The earth will shake and the shadows might cry,
tears of flowers and stars, but they still dance,
singing joys of rage knowing they will be,
together even when their shadows fade.

Shadows hand and hand may shine in the light,
under the cold branches of the elm tree,
hoping to keep the shadows warm, thinking,
forever and ever the two will be.

One day the sun may burn bright like their smiles
forcing the poor shadows to flee and run,
ending the dark dance, but always they will be
together even when their shadows fade.

But sadly now the moon cries for the loss
of the shadows whose time ran out, praying,
forever and ever the two will be
together even when their shadows fade.

Let's Talk....

I wrote this poem as a healing poem. It was a poem to help me grieve, but even more than that, it was a poem to help me live. Many times, especially in my community, there are heavy burdens placed upon young men of color. There are expectations of how you must talk, act, dress, what you can and can't aspire to be, and the list goes on. For much of my life, I fell into those societal traps until I realized it was okay for me to have moments of weakness. It took a while to recognize that those moments even existed, but looking back now, they ultimately are what made me stronger. In other words, until I was able to recognize my own flaws and limitations, I couldn't see exactly what I was capable of and who I was capable of becoming. I was spending too much time trying to conceal the aspects of my identity that I wanted to change: my high pitched voice, my love of reading, my inability of playing sports, etc. Instead of focusing on these things as characteristics that made me a strong, unique young man, I was trying to run away from them.

Today when I read this poem, I can now admit I cry. This poem, unbeknownst to me at the time, was the start of my healing process that I so desperately needed.

A city from tears

My city was born,

from the tears of the young.

Slow.

Steady.

Loud.

Impatient.

Filled with hopes that will always fly,

and dreams that will never leave the ground.

Beat boxes,

jump ropes,

men searching through trash cans

to quench their thirst.

That's my city.

A city where art is displayed on sidewalks

not in museums.

Where music pulses through the veins of the living,

and jump starts the bodies of the victims of no rhythm.

My city is filled with break dancers,

filthy streets,

gardens of teddy bears,

and chalk outlines struck frozen

next to pictures of casualties of an endless war.

I live where children are armed right out of the womb,

where the elderly wear glasses

to see the shadows of their past,

and the sun never sets.

I come from a place of immortality,

of kings and queens shrouded in darkness.

A place where time is just another body in the street,

and death walks hand and hand with life.

My city is plastered with smiles,

and it rains stars every night.

Where love is everywhere, but impossible to see,

and my city is growing.

It thrives off of the souls of the ambitious,

it thrives from the imagination of every age,

there are no limits my city can't break,

and no worlds it can't explore,

for my city was born

from the tears of a child.

Let's talk....

I grew up in the city of Brotherly Love and Sisterly affection, aka, the great city of Philadelphia. However, I saw Philly in a different light than most people. I didn't see the tourist attractions, the beautiful college campuses, the flourishing businesses of South Street and Center City. What I saw were mothers struggling to put food on their tables for their families. I saw more memorials on corners then I saw open businesses. I have been to more funerals in my short twenty years of living than most people have been to in their entire lives. I have been the victim of assault. I have had friends get caught in the cross fires of shoot outs and have been shot at. I am not asking for sympathy, nor am I saying Philly is a bad city. I am merely stating the reality I lived and grew up in.

Now, though, let me point out how powerful and beautiful people's perception of things can be. When people ask me whether or not Philly is safe, I will almost always say, "Philly is a unique place with some of the most unique people you will ever meet in your life." I believe that despite all the negativity surrounding most inner city environments, beauty can be seen in any community.

The high school I attended was an all-boys school that had developed both a positive and negative reputation in the community. Despite what the community thought about the school, the students, teachers and administrators saw the potential and beauty in the school. The struggle for most of us was taking public transportation, and the busses would not stop if they saw us at the bus stop. They would drive right on by, forcing many of us to walk home, not always a favorable option. One day, this man, about mid-thirties, was waiting on the corner for the bus with us. He overheard some of the boys talking about how the busses sometimes wouldn't stop which I guess triggered something in him. As the bus became visible down the street, this man stood in the middle of the street, blocking the flow of traffic and the bus. He stood there demanding the bus driver open the doors for us. He said it was not fair that the actions of a few should become the consequence of many. I will never forget that man. Sometimes it is the smallest acts of kindness that make me love Philly that much more.

Stories like this happen all the time here in Philadelphia, but sadly, are constantly overshadowed with stories of hatred and violence. The stories of the disabled mother who worked under the table jobs for six years so that her son could go to catholic school. The former alcoholic and drug user turned clean, who now helps other struggling people in their community. The teacher with a PHD in Science, who instead of making a higher salary by being a college professor, decided to stay in the inner city and help the generations of tomorrow. The young mother who dresses up as a clown and performs show after show in order to provide for her children. The father who worked hours and hours every day until the day he died, so that his family would never have to struggle like he did. Those are the stories I love and those are the stories and people that continue to motivate me. I didn't grow up thinking about fairy tales or dreaming of superheroes – I was surrounded by them. The sound of jump ropes hitting the concrete pavement on a Saturday morning, block parties on almost every street, jumping in the water hydrants, chalking the sidewalks for hours, laughing, smiling, enjoying the community. Those are the things that make up my community, and to me, my community will always be beautiful.

Suicide Sight

I went to the suicide slums

to see what awaited me.

There I saw a knife on the ground

with blood all around like a red sea.

 I went to the suicide slums

waiting for something to catch my eye,

when I saw a baby on her lap

fighting to stay alive.

I went to the suicide slums

expecting a miracle.

There I saw two angry birds

going mad and hysterical.

I went to the suicide slums

hoping to find me,

instead I returned with a wife

and a heart filled with glee.

I went to the suicide slums

not knowing what will be.

There I had a vision,

but it was not about me.

I went to the suicide slums

expecting to surely die,

but instead found a new take on life

and beauty finally seen through weary eyes.

For the sake of Love

I don't want another friend.
I don't want another number to sit in my phone
Hanging from the branches
Of unjustified tendencies
Like fruit
Hanging from the forbidden tree
Isolated in the Garden of Eden
Praying another curious mind will pass it by
And sink their teeth in deep

I don't want another scar
Lining my skin
Sinking into my veins
Causing my adrenaline levels to spike
As if I am shooting the sins of my past
Into my bloodstream
And getting high
Off of my own insecurities

I don't want to be addicted to pain
Like smokers to cigarettes
Huffing and puffing their way to their own death
All the while saying "that feels good"

I don't want to be soaking wet
Running from place to place
Praying that I can find shelter

From this storm pouring from my eyes
Shaking my very soul
Causing my dreams to die
Every time I reach out to grab them
And save them from being washed away
As if my fingers were on fire
And my dreams paper thin

I'm willing to give up what I love for the one I love
Even if the very thing I love is her
The one who made my heart melt
Every time I spoke her name
The one who counted my scars
And would kiss me for everyone I had

That's the one
The one I love
And you know I don't want another friend
I don't want another number to sit in my phone
Hanging from the branches
Of unjustified tendencies
Like fruit
Hanging from the forbidden tree
Isolated in the Garden of Eden
Praying another curious mind will pass it by
And sink their teeth in deep
So let me be like snow white
And take the first bite

Let's Talk....

This poem is a thank you and an I love you to the one person I met who truly understands what it means to be me. This poem, at the time I wrote it, was my way of telling her, "Hey, for the first time in a long time I have found someone who truly understands me. As much as I love having you as a friend, I want more. I want to share my life with you – the good and the bad, even if that means I have to make myself vulnerable to do so." It is not easy finding someone who accepts you and all the baggage you bring, but beyond that, it is even harder finding someone willing to sit down and help you unpack that baggage so that you can let go of it and find peace. I was lucky to have found that exact type of person, and she will always hold a special place in my heart. Today, she and I are just friends, but, in many ways, I think that is exactly what I needed the most at that time and even now. Perhaps one day we will be something more than friends, but until then, I am thankful for just being able to have her apart of my life.

Feed us

I was hungry,
searching for something to nourish my soul.
My stomach rumbled,
flipped,
turned,
wanted to be fed,
but I could not force myself to eat
so I starved…

She was hungry,
devouring everything in her path.
She was like a dream,
a muse,
then she ate from the forbidden tree.
She learned too much,
knew too much.
She was afraid to ever eat again.

He was hungry.
He was surrounded by food,
waiting to be eaten,
consumed,
but he didn't want it,
so he let it rot away.

They are hungry,
looking for food to eat.
Begging,
wishing,

praying to be fed,
for an opportunity to come,
but none ever came,
so they sat there
waiting
waiting
waiting
waiting...

They say we aren't hungry,
but if they only knew
we are hungry
starving,
wishing,
waiting,
wanting to be nourished,
but can't eat,
afraid to eat,
won't eat,
don't know how to eat,
don't have anything to eat,
so we starve....

<u>Flowers for the dead</u>

Too soon was my life taken.
Call me a martyr,
the scream that broke the silence.

Must we die for you to see,
the worth in our life.
In life, you called us nothing.

Give me my flowers before,
before I am dead,
cause in death I can't smell them.

<u>My Angel</u>

My angel,
where have you fallen to?
Don't cry, my child,
failure is inevitable
and yet…
as we fall
we must spread our wings
extend them fully
and let the wind get caught beneath them
and raise us
raise us
raise us,
then watch us fly.

But I see his fear,
he trembles
gasping for breath
in and out
in and out
breathe my child,
breathe.

He crawls on the ground,
his wings dragging behind him in the dirt,
scared to stand,
scared of what's to come,
what's next,
the future.

He cries
and yet…
he stands
tears falling
hands clenched.
He closes his eyes
and jumps
hoping the wind will catch him.

He took the leap and spread his wings,
he has made his move,
he is falling
falling
falling
falling
but-
wait—look,
lets watch him fly.

Bad to the bone

I am stuck in the night.
I take a step,
Creaaaak…
snap!!
Creaaaak
pop!
Creaaaak
Creaaaak
Creaaaak…
I'm coming.
My bones are black,
undesired
yet strong.
Creaaaak
Snap!

My bones rattle
Shake…
Creak…
Rattle…
You've tried to escape me,
ignore me,
but I am reaching out of the darkness
trying to touch you,
and you will never see me coming.

Don't be afraid of me,
old friend.
Love me,
embrace me,
forgive me.
I take a step,
Creaaaak…
snap!!
Creaaaak
pop!
Creaaaak
Creaaaak
Creaaaak…
Then let me live,
or I will die.

How I sing my joy

Am I allowed to say it?
Will it make me weak?
Can I call you by name,
pain,
hurt,
love,
anger,
no, no, no,
that's not your name.
Why can't I remember your name?
I see people who know you,
proud to claim you as a friend—
be my friend,
but what if----
If I say I know you,
must I let go of my past,
my identity…
will my struggle not be valid,
my words never be heard.

You scare me,
captivate me,
love me,
hate me,
are a mystery to me.
Are you dangerous,
for my community has exiled you,
banned you,
cursed you…
and yet they desire you,

want you,
dream about you,
wish for you,
long for your affection,
but don't know how to find you.

I imagine being free,
free to understand
what it means to be free---
free to love you,
know you,
grow with you,
share you,
care for you,
give you as a gift,
make you somebody's wish,
but I can't touch you,
lift you,
because you're not real...
only a dream
a word,
just a word.
And yet, I pray,
wish,
hope,
I am wrong,
hope you will come visit me,
tell me that you care,
that I have nothing to fear,
that you have always been here...

I guess I was just too scared to say your name.

The Perfect Picture

Cut me deep and drain me dry.

Mix my blood with pigments of your choice,

and hang what's left of me on your canvas.

Grab your paintbrush and paint what you wish to see.

Paint a smile on my face

as captivating as the Mona Lisa's,

and pray it will distract people

from the tears that fall from my blackened eyes

caused by your hateful words that sting

like needles,

jabbing,

carving into my flesh.

Make me look as lifeless as possible,

leaving my mind empty,

so you can construct in me what you wish.

Praying that this will stop me

from awakening in the night,

scrambling in the dark,

like an infant searching for some comfort,

but only finding the whited out words of your affection

that I will never see.

Create a beautiful background.

Hoping that it will help you forget about my past

that has been entwined with the lies of your tongue,

that squeeze the life out of everything they touch,

like a snake getting ready to devour its next meal.

Paint in the rest of my siblings

and cast us as the perfect family.

Let us perform the perfect show.

Silence my voice to keep me in line,

but do right by the others.

Let them cry when they feel pain

and smile when they are happy.

Do not silence their dreams

like you shackled my soul

which you keep locked away from the world,

placed high upon a shelf,

wishing that one day it will slowly fade away and die.

Now step back and look at your painting.

Admire the lie you have created.

Marvel at the shadows of pain that try to shine through.

Question the depths of my determination,

as you throw more paint

onto your masterpiece of deception,

trying to keep the lies away from the truth.

And as you struggle

to keep my raging soul from being set free,

look into my now perfect eyes

that you have created with the strokes of your hand

and tell me you love me.

That you now love this perfect picture….

Let's Talk….

I have a love-hate relationship with this poem because I wrote it about my father. However, the more I read through it, the more I realize that the poem is not actually about my father, but about a boy wishing he had a father. Don't get me wrong, I have an amazingly strong mother for whom I would lay my life down for, as well as strong male role models who have become father figures to me throughout my life, including one who I call my dad. This poem does not negate these facts. It is just a poem written by a boy who really wanted a father of his own.

Growing up, there were many times I did not think about my father at all, especially when my friends and I would discuss how proud we were of our strong, single mothers. Then there were *those* other times – times when I would see a father holding his son's hand, playing catch with him in the field, or just simply hugging and kissing his son. These were the times that made me cry. For much of my early life I thought I would never know what it meant to be a man simply because I did not have a father to show me how, one that would lead and guide me. Then one day, my life changed inexplicably: my father stepped back into my life. However, it was not for long and it was only to tell me that I had two little siblings. I was crushed. The thought of them growing up and having something I longed for, something I prayed for every night truly bothered and upset me. I remember meeting members of my dad's extended family who all shared the same reaction, "I didn't know your father had any other children." Out of my father's five children, I am the one most people do not even know exists. Even as I type this, I wonder how many of my family members may stumble across this book, read it and never know that we are related.

I wrote this poem initially out of anger, out of pure hateful anger. Yet after many years of self-reflection and self-discovery, I grew to realize that I indeed had a father this entire time. A father who held me every night before I went to sleep, a father who provided everything I needed in life, a father who inspired me and pushed me to be a better man: my father was God, and he has blessed me with some of the most brilliant, strong, passionate and caring father figures in the world. For a long time, I was so caught up in what I didn't have that I forgot to look at the blessings that I did. For those out there longing for a father figure, know you are not alone. It is a struggle dealing with the myriad of questions that constantly plague you – what did I do wrong? What can I do to fix it? What if I could change? What if I weren't born? When these questions crop up again, remember this: something can't come from nothing, but anything can come from something.

The Moon's Shepard

A time of pain

And love so sweet

Rains down

When the moon and a Sheppard meet

He sleeps so still

And quiet as he dreams

As the moon swings down

Like a golden beam

Each night she comes

And kisses his face

Painfully knowing their tragic fate

But still she sits and waits

And she waits

She pleads and weeps

For an answer so weak

To fix her heart

That day by day

Get's ripped apart

To sleep forever

Is her wish for him

To be with her love

Until his lights dim

When he passed away

From slumber so sweet

Her heart broke

And her soul made weak

But some still say

She comes to his grave

To see her lover

And his memory to save

Just take the stairs

You're so fat just take the stairs

for no one cares

about you my dear.

They don't care to see your pain

that falls to the ground

like an April rain.

They will deny

all the problems that won't let you fly,

for they rather watch you sit and cry.

But I my dear

know of your pain

that pricks your skin

and leaves tear stains.

They run down your cheeks so tender and mild

taking your innocence,

refusing to let you be a child.

I know of the nights you sat and cried,

and all of the days that you tried

to convince yourself that you lied

about the pain that has you tied

to the ground pulling you down.

Your burdens keep trying to make you drown

tearing your whole world apart

step by step

brick by brick,

until there is nothing left to make you tick.

I know your weight is not yours alone,

but nobody dares ask why you have not yet flown

across the skies high and low,

sharing with the world

your charming glow.

But I will ask of all your pain,

of all your hurt

and all your shame.

I will carry your weight too,

because you still have work to do.

So ignore the haters when they care

to loudly say their hateful share,

of you're so fat just take the stairs

for no one cares

about you my dear,

for someone does

and that someone is me,

just hold on tight

and you will soon see.

<u>Big things in small packages</u>

You may call me small,
but your world was built by me.
Black with tears all over.

You may call me weak,
but my hands saved yours from pain.
Try and do my work.

You may beat me red,
but I can endure, can you?
My skin is thick.

Hopeless I may be,
but if you really knew me…
You would be frightened.

Don't judge me blindly,
for I cost more than you think.
I can't be bought!

"I" want to be "we"

I

I want to be

I want to be me

I want to be me for you and you for me

But I can't see

I can't see you and me

You and me as we

As us

Not yet

Not until I tell you who I want be

I want to be

I want to be a clown

A clown that makes you laugh when you're sad

I want to be that song

That song that puts that twinkle in your eye

Or maybe

Maybe the moon

And you could be my sun

We could be one

We could be together forever

Now I want to be your lawyer

For even if we are dead wrong

It will still be me and you

Me and you against the world

And I want to be your knight

That knight in shining armor you dreamed about

And I

I want to fight

I want to fight monsters for you

For even if you don't believe in them they are still there

And I

I want to make sure you are safe

I want to be your pillow

When you cry so will I

I want to be your friend

A friend through thick and thin

I want to be that look

That look on your face when you're happy

 I want to be that smile

That smile

Your smile

 I want you to smile at me

Just smile at me and show me

Show me who you

Who you want me to be

For I

I want to be

I want to be me for you and you for me

And I want to see

I want to see me and you

Me and you become we

Emotions of a broken heart

As the rain slowly drips off of the leaves,

my heart burns for your affections.

Yet, I long to know if this is really true,

if it was really meant for me to be with you.

When the wind sends whispers through the air,

I question if you really want to be here.

You constantly tell me how you feel,

but words mean nothing to me honestly.

As the sun kisses the sky, I wonder why I smile…

I smile despite I want to cry,

but it's just that feeling that keeps me strong.

When the flowers open to greet the world,

I wonder why you stop and look at other beauties.

I may be blind but I am not stupid,

yet I still trust you.

The moment the skies open up and cry,

they will not be alone.

We will sit there together,

and hope to find an answer in our tears.

Love is beautiful,

but to a broken heart it seems impossible.

Yet I can't help but feel that you are trying to fix it,

and I smile at the thought of us.

The rain slowly drips off of the leaves,

the wind sends whispers through the air,

the sun kisses the sky,

the flowers open to greet the world,

the skies open up and cry,

and I am madly in love,

suffering with the emotions of a broken heart.

Sidewalks

Never-ending days,

Blistering nights

Keep me longing for something

Something more.

Like sidewalks so dear,

That twist and turn, but never really stop.

They cry from the filth

Seeping into their veins,

Wanting to be clean,

To be free.

They wish they too could walk

And not be the bearers of

Rough feet

And neglected dreams.

But until the sidewalks find their hands, face, feet,

They shall lay there,

And like them,

I too shall be captive,

Never to be free,

Walking endlessly

Filled with dreams that will never be deemed,

Deemed worthy.

The Sun Bearers Journey

Darkness falls

On the valley of the moon

As the sun bearers arise

And the day flowers bloom

For theirs is patience

Patience for a new day

Unlike those sad tumble weeds

That all have blown away

The sun bearers walk

Through the darkest of lands

To reach darker places

Of seas and sands

Each step they take

Is as blind as the next

With no pure light

To see their guided text

Look outward they don't

But inward once more

To find that faith

So they can endure

And when the sun rises

The sun bearers rest

Preparing for the next nights journey

Preparing for the next nights test

The Flood

I invited you to my table
You sat and smiled
Telling me exactly what I needed to hear
Exactly what you needed to say
Your hands like the ocean
Gentle
Calm
Trusting
Until I realized I was drowning
Crying out for help
Trying to swim to the shore of my horizon
Only to realize the sun had already set
Leaving me
Alone
Cold
Drowning in my own tears
You smiled
Kissed me on the head as if you were proud that I survived
You smiled
Admiring your work as I laid there
Lifeless
You smiled
And I fell
Fell to a place where the weak are scared to go
Where the strong go to die
And I screamed to the heavens
Pleading this flood would die
That the waters would recede
and I'd drift back to my reality as if it was all a dream
You smiled
Leaving me floating in my own tears

I invited you to my table
You sat and smiled
Telling me exactly what I needed to hear
Exactly what you needed to say
Your hands like the ocean
Gentle
Calm
Trusting
Until I realized I was drowning
Until I realized I had died
Until I realized
I lived

The Sunflower

A dreamer sits
in a field of stars,
waiting for love
from the sun so far.

She sits
with a silent tongue,
hoping one day
her love will come.

She follows his face
from east to west,
with no food and drink
and surely no rest.

She survives on tears
so bitter and sweet,
in the company of flowers
crushed under her weary feet.

Her dreams have faded
and her heart turned black,
dreaming a dream
of love sadly lacked.

When the earth rose up
to ease her pain,
she fell to its grasp
with glee unashamed.

Her feet turned to roots
and her tears to seeds,
as her body became green
and covered with leaves.

To this day
our lover still waits
following the sun
waiting patiently for her mate.

Inhale: A Prayer for Sandy Hook

My breath is not my own
for I breathe with lungs pierced by bullets
that used to belong to a little girl no older than five.

My hands tremble,
for they are the hands of a scared little boy
who never knew what pain was
until it crept through his veins,
grasping him by the waist and never letting go.

My tears are from the mothers and fathers
who wish death had kissed their lips instead.
For the heroes who threw themselves into the fire,
letting their voices be the fuel for the eternal flames
that proclaimed its victims would never die
even when they stopped burning.

And each prayer that slips through my lips,
never knowing they escaped
until my heart hits E,
came from the heavens
sung by the heavenly host weeping of pain,
yet rejoicing in hope,
trying to remind us that the heavens cry too,
but not for the dead, but for the living.

And with each passing hour,
I pray the pain will ease,
although the scars may remain for eternity.

Let my love be free

I once called you my prince

and we danced upon the snow.

You held me tight and said you would never let me go,

but your arms were weak

and my heart to thin,

so you let me blow away

never to see me again.

I once called you my hero

and you caused me my life,

for a hero is no hero

when he craves your blood

and takes your life.

One day I asked you to be my wife,

you smiled

kissed me and said yes with delight.

The wedding was beautiful, but too bad you was not there.

I stood there in tears

while you slowly disappeared.

You said you was my queen

and I kissed your feet with glee,

until the day I opened my eyes to see

that he had already replaced me.

But today I call to myself

asking to be free,

for being alone does not mean I am lonely.

When I cry it does not mean I am sad,

for my wings are still flapping

and I am going for the ride,

until my heart can love again

and I can say I love who I am.

Freedom

They tell me slavery is over,
yet I'm still a prisoner on this plantation you call home.
I smile,
say please and thank you,
call you master
and bow down low.
Maybe if I bend down low enough
I'll finally be able to hit the ground,
cause it feels like I just keep falling,
and falling,
and falling,
and I rather be pressed against the earth
smacked down to the ground
by your back handed compliments
then to live in this nightmare.
Excuse me,
I meant your dreams coming true.
They tell me I am free,
yet instead of living my dreams
I am picking yours off the ground,
as if I am picking cotton from the fields,
one after the other
until my hands bleed,
my knees buckle,
And I finally fall.
Fall!
Fall, hard on the ground

wishing you won't see me.
But you do.

Forcing your existence onto me,
raping my soul,
bending my back,
pressing deep into my spine
like whips,
ripping at my flesh.
They cut deep into my skin,
reminding me that this must be what freedom is,
because they tell me I can leave.
I can walk.
Run.
Fly.
Escape.
Yet I stay!
We stay.
Scared…
Scared of this word called freedom.
Looking out into the fields
that produce more dead bodies then crops,
all hoping,
crying,
fighting,
trying to find freedom.
They tell me slavery is over,
and that I am free.
Well somebody needs to go and tell freedom
because obviously
Freedom has forgotten me.

<u>Nursery Rhyme</u>

The itsy bitsy spider went up the waterspout,

down came the rain and washed the spider out.

Out came the sun and dried up all the rain,

and the itsy bitsy spider went up the spout again

again

again

and again

just like a child

your child

because you are my sun

and whenever the sun came

I knew you were there to save me

be brave for me

teach me

keep me.

You kept your patience when I lost my head

holding me

scolding me

loving me

having fun with me

and then one day I grew up,

as if right before your eyes,

and you said I was your sun,

that I brightened your day,

but when I was sexually assaulted

lost

scared

hurt

you was my sun,

drying up the down pour of rain dripping from my eyes

you was my sun,

 my mother.

When I was sick

lying in bed

no cure

no clue

no doctors with answers

only you.

You stayed

prayed

laid hands on me

and now you will see

I am my mothers child,

mommas boy.

Strong like my mom

sweet

nurturing

caring

gentle like a lamb

fierce like a lion

my mother…..

When I said goodbye

both our hearts broke

shattered

will they ever be put back together?

Be able to endure this ever changing whether?

But mom this poem is for you

I love you

thank you

I owe you

but my debt is to huge to pay

but I will try everyday

everyway

I love you

your gentle but strong hands

constructed

molded

rocked me to sleep every night.

Your eyes that have seen me grow

seen me go

seen me come back

give back

love back

your strength

a strong black women

single mother

Queen.

I want to make you happy,

Proud of me.

Even as I write this poem,

I know it can't say how much

I admire you

love you

I'll give you your flowers while I still can.

These flowers are my thanks,

my life,

my love

you are the greatest gift from above

above

like the sun

my sun

my light

my mom....

The itsy bitsy spider went up the waterspout,

down came the rain and washed the spider out.

Out came the sun and dried up all the rain,

and the itsy bitsy spider went up the spout again.

~This poem is dedicated to my beautiful, powerful and supporting mother. Many people say it is impossible for a women to raise a "real man", but I challenge them to look at me. You have made me who I am and I love you so much. I'm thankful that God has blessed me with you as my mother, and I look forward to the many years God has planned for us together. I love you always and forever.~

Rise for tomorrow

We cry to the heavens
Praying for a change
Walking that long dusty road
Chained and forgotten

We walk silently to the tables
Thankful for the food we have to eat
With a simple loaf of bread
We all take our seats

We wash in the river
And sleep on the ground
It's hard to complain
When there is no one willing to listen around

Soon we will walk
With the chains unlocked
Still praying to the heavens
For a change to come

Our houses are beautiful
So clean and neat
But we sacrifice our own health
So that our children have enough food to eat

We wash with warm water
And sleep in beds

But worries of tomorrow
Will never leave our heads

Though times have changed
Our worries are still real
The struggle is not over
But it will never break our will

Soon there won't be tears to cry
But our prayers will never go away
For soon our struggles will be over
And we will rejoice in the new day

Be you

They called me beautiful,

I was beautiful,

black was beautiful,

I was me.

They called me ugly,

tore my children from my arms

and dared me to cry.

Can you still see my beauty?

They called us free.

Free to go where?

Free to die?

Maybe I will be beautiful dead?

They called us worthless,

to lazy to do anything,

but smart enough to do nothing.

This beauty must be a curse.

They call you my child.

I call you beautiful,

for black is beautiful

and now you are free to be beautiful.

Beautiful….

Beauty…

I wish you knew what you cost.

To our tree

I once had a tree
that said I was its sun.
It spoke to me and told me stories
as I danced around its trunk
surrounded by morning glories.
It shed its bark,
and cut off its leaves.
And from the two
it weaved me a basket
saying,
I will never go.

But today,
I hold the basket close to my heart,
filled with morning glories.
I walk the road of silent prayers
to your wooden casket.
Whispering, I will never go.
We will never go.

Let's Talk....

This poem is the most difficult to talk about; not because I hate the poem, but purely because it requires me to talk about emotions that I have not fully come to grips with. In 2010, my sophomore year of high school, my life was changed forever. This poem is dedicated to two of the most influential people in my life who have passed: my grandmother and uncle.

My grandmother was diagnosed with Alzheimer's in 2010, and was eventually diagnosed with several other health problems that she struggled with until the day she passed on. When someone you love is sick, you never want to come to terms with it and that is exactly how I was. People would always say that my grandmother was forgetting things and that she should be put in a nursing home, but I did not want to believe it. However, that all changed on one singular day during our weekly lunch outing after church. On this day, we were heading to the restaurant, as usual, when, in a split second, she forgot how to drive: we were in the middle of rush hour, in a city, in a high-volume traffic area. My heart stopped. Not because we could have died, but because I had to finally come to terms with the fact that my grandmother was truly sick. Every time I saw my grandmother after that moment, I was confronted with the reality that slowly but surely my grandmother was losing her memory, memories that comprised all of our time together: weekly lunch outings, monthly coffee and doughnut outings, Christmas traditions of eating Cream of Chicken soup while drinking milkshakes and watching Christmas movies. The first time I saw my grandmother in the nursing home, I had no idea who she was. This was the woman who helped raise me for the better part of my sixteen years of life, and she had gotten so sick that I did not even know who she was. And that crushed me more than anything else.

Four years later, my sophomore year of college, I received an unexpected phone call that also changed my life. Security called my cell phone telling me to call home; I hadn't noticed my phone ringing all morning. When I returned the call, my sister was crying and gasping for breath in order to tell me the news: my Uncle Kevin had just been in a car accident and was dead. I fell to the ground in tears, screaming. This was my uncle, the man who took the place of my father. I remember a time when he was the only person standing at the ready, willing to fight for me, trying to protect me from all the evil, negative, bitter people who were constantly trying to tear me down and hurt me. People who wanted to rip my poetry up in front of a 10 year old boy telling him he would never amount to shit. People who threw me against walls, all the while screaming and yelling in my face. He was there when I was sexually assaulted as a child, jumped and had my phone taken from me, scared, lost, hurting, hated myself, struggling to find my place in the world, succeeding, failing. He stood there protecting a small scared child who was not even related to him, and yet, he told me I will always be his nephew until the day he died. He was my hero. My rock. My uncle. The only person I had ever looked at as a father. And I was just told he was dead.

I done a lot of healing since those times, but there are days when I still cry about not having my uncle or my grandmother in my life. I don't have some secret remedy about healing or letting go of those who have passed away, and I probably never will. All I can say is this: my grandmother used to always tell me nothing beats a failure except a try. My uncle used to tell me that we have to learn how to dance during our storms, otherwise we'd be waiting all our lives for our sun to reappear. When I reflect on both of those things I come to the conclusion that we will have problems, and during these times, it seems as if our storm will never stop. However, we have to be willing to take a chance, dance in the midst of our storms, laugh in the face of trouble, smile through our pain, and have fun when our world is crumbling, or we will always be sitting around just waiting. So, take a chance, make mistakes, fall, fail, cry, struggle, but keep living because nothing will ever beat a failure except a try and that's all I am doing. I'm just trying.

Phoenix: The legacy of Matches

They say you smell the smoke before you see the flames, so let me strike this match. Watch as the smoke rises into the air. Do you notice me now, or am I not transparent enough? Transparent. The word I tried to be for you, for us. There was a time I burned all my bridges thinking it was wise to be too safe then naïve. You told me to trust you, love you, and let my bridges remain. I left them alone. You crossed my bridges as if they belonged to you. Destroying them, rebuilding them, telling me you could improve them. Trying to reinforce them with faulty promises, fake whispers of prosperity, and rusted old screws that crumble under the slightest touch. I sat there watching, waiting, and wishing I had just burnt them. Strike another match, let the igniter burst into existence and slowly consume the matchstick. Consume. That's all fire is known to do, consume, destroy, hurt, and yet it was fire that fueled my passion for you. Consumed my life like a raging sea, scorching everything in its path until all that was left was a burning sea of flames and beauty, until I looked. My dreams, my life, used to fuel these burning flames. Ash and dust. Dust and ash is all that is left. I strike another match praying things will get better, and another and another, five, six, seven. They burn. Encircling me in a ring of fire and I sit there smiling. Perhaps these flames can burn brighter and brighter, leading me out of this darkness, like the sun bursting through the night sky, giving way to the day. Giving way to life. Life. I remember what it felt like to live.

They say you smell the smoke before you see the flames, so I lite my matches hoping people would smell the signs of trouble before it was too late. But it was too late. Consumed in their own selfish desires, needs, wants. They let me sit there, crying, and screaming for help, burning. I tried to ask for help, but just like a match they let me burn until there was nothing left but ash.

Ash.

And yet…

I Speak.

Let's Talk....

There is an extreme amount of hurt and pain wrapped up inside of this poem. Long story short, I thought I was in love. I gave the person everything and for a while it seemed as if we were going to be together for a long time. Admittedly, I should have seen the signs. First off, my family hated this person. Second, we were not ready for this thing called love or even knew what love was. Heck, I still don't know what it is entirely, but I do know what it is not. This realization led me to the third sign – the truth. There were so many things I wanted and needed to say to this individual, but could not muster up the strength or courage to do so. When I finally did have the courage to confront them, I realized that our relationship was already on fire, and everything that we rushed so quickly to build was slowly burning and turning to ashes. So we broke up and stopped talking. Afterwards, I tried reaching out to this person several times and was rejected every time. Truth of the matter is I'm glad. My grandmother used to always say never burn a bridge and she was right. Some bridges just rot and decay and eventually fall apart on their own. Once the bridge is gone, then it is up to the builder to decide what to do. Leave it alone, rebuild the bridge, or create something new from the ashes. I chose the latter. I chose to give myself a second chance.

I Dare

Each year we pray
for something new,
something exciting,
something true.

At the stroke of twelve
we scream and cheer,
hoping our wishes
will magically appear.

There are things we never dream about,
things we never say,
because nobody ever to us we could.
Nobody ever invited our dreams to stay.

But this year
I dare to dream,
I dare to smile,
I dare my dreams to stay a while.

I have found a love I know to be true,
a soul born a new,
a heart I will cherish to the end,
a new love,

a new best friend.

I found my dreams
that I thought had died,
hopes forgotten,
love tossed aside.

Each year we pray
for something new,
something exciting,
something true.

There are things we never dream about,
things we never say.
Because nobody ever told us we could.
Nobody ever invited our dreams to stay.

At the stroke of twelve
I'll scream and cheer,
knowing that all my dreams
are already here.

The End to a beginning

He lays there on the floor.

His hands move, but his heart is still.

Tears flood his face,

mixing with the ink from his pen,

as the two blend together on his paper.

Memories of

long nights on the phone,

cheers and laughter at lunch,

arguments and fights,

hugs,

sleepless nights,

friendships,

begin to take form,

like flowers blossoming,

reminding him

that change is in the air.

A change that can melt the coldest of hearts,

and bring life to the dead.

A change that leaves him

lying on the floor,

searching for his last words

before he dies in one world

and born into another.

But nothing comes.

The thought of being dead in two worlds

never reaches his soul,

for his mind is lost,

trying to see through a fog so thick

that it burns

 leaving him scared,

oblivious to the reality of dreams

he has surrounded himself in.

His dreams causes him to lose track of who he is,

or who he wants to be,

leaving only an empty shell,

a broken container of flesh and bones

that wants to live,

wants to feel,

wants to break away from all the forced fed lies

of failure and pain.

Hoping for just one night,

to experience joy and loving memories,

to taste sweet tears of success,

and scream cries of happiness.

Never worrying about the fear of tomorrow

or revenges nasty grip reaching out from the day before.

So he lies there

on that cold icy floor

and lets his hands move,

as the tears flow,

hoping that his heart will beat again

so that he too can be free.

Our Feet are on the ground

My ancestors once hung from trees, suspended off the ground like trophies on a shelf. We were burnt so that people could dance to the rhythm of our cries. Today, my people don't even the fuck exist. We have no home, no place to call mine. We were tied together and burnt so that my ancestors of the past could have a place to burn. Being gay is hard enough, but being a gay black kid is suicide. Now a days we retreat to our closets hoping that being closeted will keep us safe, not realizing that our safe havens will turn into our coffins as we hang there. We hang ourselves before others can hang us and tell stories of how they used our bones for toothpicks. Why the FUCK did God make me gay and black was it a joke, because either way someone was going to hang me or I hang myself.

Sometimes I wish people could see that I bleed red. I bleed red. Not sprinkles and sparkles, neither group I identify with means that I have FUCKING aids, and you sure the FUCK can't judge my worth from it. So try it. Grab your hands and use your forked tongues like you do to me and cut yourself and see what the fuck color you bleed. If by chance we bleed the same color will you then see that success is color blind and love holds no discrimination. Now justice may be a little bit biased, but if you go and knock on Karmas door she will tell you she can be a bitch.

It's ironic that today we claim the rainbow. In biblical terms the rainbow was a sign of Gods promise never to destroy the earth again by the flood. Yet here we are, drowning in these waters that keep on rising. They call this the sea of tears. Our dead bodies just another casualty of war. Fools holding onto empty promises who realized to late that their promises, their rainbows, must have been an exclusionary deal.

So let your words fly like bullets ready to kill us. We will watch as they fall to our feet and we will step on them and carefully listen as they are crushed under the weight of our existence for we are here. WE are here. WE ARE HERE!

My people once hung from trees suspended off the ground like trophies on a shelf, but now our feet are on the ground.

~This poem is written and dedicated to a close friend of mine. Despite what people say to you, or about you, you know who you are and you know you are blessed. Keep your mustard seed faith, keep praying and keep pushing forward my friend.

We are standing
we rise
like tress
strong
unmoving
secure
we rise
like birds
soaring
exploring
controlling our own paths
we rise
like the stars
mysterious
unchanging
breath taking
we rise
like the tide
creeping
slowly
and slowly higher until
we rise
for we rise
like the first flower of Spring
nourished
strong
delicately made
beautifully designed
ready
waiting for the right time
the right moment
then
we rise

The Shadows that dance across the stage

In a blur of movement
not seen since the beginning of age.

Two total,
totally different rhythms,
bond and become one
under the cooling sun.

One follows the other
as the shadows merge
then separate
and return,
but never too late.

Never knowing which step is next,
never knowing the next turn,
they reach in unison
with nothing but the world to win.

and once they think it's over
they leave,
only to dream of the next dance
the two shadows will conceive.

Four Words

Hands scratching at the table. Bleeding through clenched eyes, tongue burning, thoughts racing. Feet pressed into the ground as if they were roots trying to hold me to reality. Trying to brace me, as four words begin to etch themselves into my existence, as if it was a scar that I must be forever ashamed of. Niggers are the worse! Niggers are the worse!! Niggers are the worse!!! Now forever etched into my skin. Panic and shame, shame and panic, panic and shame, shame of what?

Ashamed that my skin is laced with pigments as rich as the earth we come from? Ashamed that my tongue rejects a language so familiar, yet so foreign to my soul. Trying to learn words like syrup instead of syrp, shrimp instead of scrimp, three instead of tree, purse instead of pocket book, faggot instead of son, retard instead of friend, nigger instead of uncles. Nigger instead of aunts, mother, father, sister, brother, cousins. Me! Ashamed that my stomach begins to twist and turn at the first bite of food. Bracing the table even harder. Feeling sick. Feeling scared. My stomach is rejecting the very thing keeping me alive, as if my body is begging me to let go. As if my body wants to rid my soul of this tainted graffiti brutally forced upon it. Hoping that my soul could be free. Be free. Be me. To walk among my ancestors, lifting our voices and feeling our skin as if it is the first time we are proud of who we are. The first time we ever saw the color black. The first time we realized our beauty. Ashamed of the voices screaming in the night about injustice, yet ignoring their realities when the lights come on. But what of the people who can't escape the night, for night is their skin and their realities? Do we act as if they don't exist, or embrace them and let night consume us too? Ashamed that I let four words determine my worth, stopping me from seeing how valuable I truly am. We truly are. My skin is dark, tongue is foreign, my soul is crying to go home, but I stand firm for my feet are still pressed against the ground like roots supporting me, and my hands are still gripping the table. Strong. Sturdy. And my soul is longing to go home. Longing to be free. I open my eyes and smile.

I'm here,

I'm strong,

I'm home,

I'm free.

Let's Talk....

This poem is one that I wish I never had to write, but the truth is, eventually, it would have gotten written. I remember growing up and hearing my grandmother, mother, aunts and uncles all talking about racism. As a child, I thought it was something that no longer existed, and if it did, it only existed in small, isolated communities – communities I never thought I would cross paths with. I remember when the security report went out labeling the event as a "bias incident". I scrolled through the email crying the whole time. Somebody had written "Niggers are the worse" on a public board in a student residency hall. For days I walked around guarded, scared if you will. Not scared of being attacked or hurt, but simply scared because that message could have been written by anybody on my campus. For all I knew I could be standing in line with them, in class with them, high fiving them in the hallway, and that thought alone scared me.

Conversations about the incident took place all over campus. This poem was written after engaging in one of those conversations during a talk about intersectionality. As we went around the room talking about the incident, the common response kept being thrown out was, "It happens". After about the sixth time I got really frustrated.

It is not that these things don't happen, because they do, and more frequently than it should. It was the fact that people are just saying "it happens" and brushing it off as if it was nothing at all. This poem was a response to all those people who actually thought that saying "it happens" was an appropriate response. Yes, racism does happen, but just ignoring racist acts and doing nothing about them is not an appropriate response. Before college racism was just a concept that I read about in text books, but now it is something that I have dealt with more times than I can count. This poem was a way of me trying to find a right response to everything that was going on during that time period. To be honest, I don't know what the right response is; however, for me, this poem was the closest thing I could get.

Even today when I am the victim of racism or see racist acts occurring, I tend to just read this poem. It is a reminder that, despite whatever people think about me, my race, etc., I am still here, a successful and highly blessed young man, and I cannot be stopped. The road may be difficult but I am thankful. My ancestors marched, bled, died, strived, and persevered through many years of discrimination. Although much progress has been made, there is still a lot of hatred and hurt in this world. Every day when I wake up, I think about my past, then I look towards the future. I think about my ancestors and then I look at my legacy, my nieces, little cousins, my future kids and I keep going. As my ancestors have paved the road for me, I wish to pave the road for future generations. Know that despite your circumstance you are loved and are not alone. Be strong like a tree, because even if all your leaves fall off and your branches break, your roots run deep and they are strong. Be strong like roots and you will never have to question your place or your purpose in this world because you will know exactly where you belong. Because you do belong.

New Love

A new baby

A new joy

A new gift

A blessed baby girl

The joys of life

showed through her smile.

Peace will be found

in the laughter you will share,

and love will always be carried around

in your heart with care.

Time may slip

day by day,

but surely ya'll most precious trip

will be to watch her grow and play

from a sweet child

to a teenager so mild.

Soon an adult she will be,

the world all hers to explore and see,

but the love you share will never go

instead year by year only grow.

Her smile will always outshine the sun.

Her little hands and toes,

as sweet and innocent as freshly fallen snow

will reach out and touch your soul

to remind you of the joys that follows a storm,

no matter how old

for the innocence of her love

will be like Noah's most sacred dove.

Your new baby girl

sacred to the world she shall be.

She will save humanity

with one smile at a time,

the softness of her voice,

the pureness of her mind,

the calmness in her eyes,

the love in your heart,

and the love in hers

will withstand the test of time.

A new baby

A new joy

A new gift

A blessed baby girl.

This poem is dedicated to my niece and her amazingly
strong mother. I love ya'll both so much.

Humpty Dumpty

You called me a classic,

like a fairy tale,

indestructible.

You said I was forged by the hands of time,

and I believed you.

But classic means to be treasured

not to be treated like treasure---

used,

hidden,

kept secret,

not from love, but lustful desire.

Kept atop a wall to be admired for my value,

but never valued.

I tried to walk-

my feet confined,

one steady step after another.

Slow.

Trying to walk atop this narrow wall.

You said you will bring me to new places,

shield,

protect,

guard me,

so I jumped,

hoping you would notice....

Many of kings have tried,

Queens arrived,

Doctors lied,

but nobody could put me back together again,

and they never can

because I didn't break....

I will never be broken.

The color Red

The ceiling is stained
where the blood dripped down,
down to the floor.
There forever,
and ever more.

When words ran rampant
and fears became great,
where nothing seemed right
and hope arrived late.

Cries and screams
broke free of their chains,
as blood poured down
like a storming rain.

It moved like lava
destroying everything in its path,
taking many lives
with its destructive wrath.

Now, the blood
has settled in,
making room for despair
and an unseen fear.

And now the ceiling is stained
where the blood dripped down,
down to the floor.
There forever,
and ever more.

Love Conquers

Aphrodite's stars
danced across the night sky,
bringing romance from afar
and hope into wandering eyes.

A simple invitation
led to an inviting kiss.
Unaware of future complications,
captivated in time's bliss.

Fates call
can leads hearts in different ways,
but love is the cure-all
and never strays.

When the muses song
is heard by death ears,
it is never too long
till two hearts find one life to share.

And as the year ends
Aphrodite's stars appear,
letting hearts know a new life begins
with four simple words "I do my dear".

Fruitless

I stood there,
trying,
to pick fruit from trees consumed by deaths icy kiss.
Admiring their withered form,
worried if I leave
what I would miss…

He stands there
Frozen
Trying to pick my fruit
Not knowing I was sleep
Resting
Dead
Fruitless
Until his form began to wither
And now I wonder
What did he miss
Waiting for me to bloom

Let's Talk….

This poem is two-fold. I absolutely love and hate this poem. I love this poem because it is exactly what I need to hear, a lot, but I also hate it because it's what I need to hear a lot. I'd like to start with the former because talking about the positive is easy. I love this poem because it reminds me to take risk, make mistakes and keep trying. There's a saying that my grandmother used to say which is, "prayer without work and faith is useless". You can pray to God as hard and as long as you want, but unless you believe in what you are praying for and know what change you are working towards, then nothing will happen. That is how I try and approach life. However, it took me a while to get there. When I wrote this poem I was sitting around just waiting. Waiting for a relationship, a job, finances, health; I was just waiting. Stagnant. I had developed a crush on someone and despite the fact that I knew they were only interested in being friends, I still kept waiting and hoping for something to happen. It wasn't until I figuratively woke up, took a look around and realized that the world, my life, was still going on around me, even though I had stopped being hungry and passionate about my future.

However, I also hate this poem. There are many times when I get too complacent and become comfortable in my situation. Everything around me becomes "normalized" and I'm okay with it. It took a conversation with a wise lady who once told me that one day I will look back on my past and see that what was normal for me during that time was not actually normal at all, it was ordinary; how I handled situations and obstacles in my life and the experiences I chose to have is what would make my story *extra*ordinary.   I didn't quite understand it at the time, but looking back, now I do. During the time I wrote this poem I missed out on a lot of great opportunities. I didn't take a chance with relationships because I was afraid my heart would break, I was scared to take leadership roles because I didn't know if people would follow me, I was afraid of growing up because I didn't want to lose my childhood, I was just afraid and now I know that's normal. Being afraid was not the problem; it was the fact that I let fear control my life that was the problem. I wrote this poem as a reminder of the beauty and the dangers of waiting. Yes, waiting and being patient can produce amazing and beautiful results: waiting to see if your child is going to be a boy or a girl, waiting to see if you passed that painstaking exam, waiting to see if all your hard work paid off at your job, in your relationship, etc. However, sometimes if you wait too long and just sit there trying the same thing over and over again, hoping for new results, well, that's when you go insane. If you want an apple from a tree, but the tree does not have any apples you have two options: you can sit and wait for the tree to give you apples only to realize it's an orange tree, or you can go find another way to get your apples. The choice was mine to either be like the boy waiting on the tree to give it something it could never give, or be like the tree wondering why the boy didn't leave. I chose neither....

Untitled

I'm sorry. I guess you hear that a lot from me now a days, but it's because I am. Sometimes I forget that it's not just your milk chocolate skin that makes you a target in this world, but your long hair, painted nails, curled eyelashes, and woman hood that must make you seem almost apocalyptic. It's funny because the very thing we take pride in you for is also the thing we criticize you the most about. Your beauty.

Now a days we want you to live up to certain expectations, but once you begin to blossom beyond what we like, we try to cut you off at your roots hoping that you will now depend on us to help you grow. And when I say us it goes beyond the typical hormonal driven robots that operate depending on how high their testosterone levels are that day. When I say us I mean anyone who has ever put you down, hurt or abused you. Anyone who has ever talked about you thinking they know you, but are obviously oblivious to the fact that we made you who you are. We dressed you up as if you were our personal doll that we can manipulate into doing whatever we want. We turned your silky smooth black hair into our own personal garden, planting whatever flowers we thought would make you look the most stunning. We even went as far as covering your face with our own masterpieces, thinking that if you looked at it long enough you would be forced into believing it. And you were. Now when I look at you I can't see you. I can't see who you were or who I know you still are. All I can do now is try to sort through my memories trying to figure out what's real and what I imagine to be real. Is your smile real, or is it something I wish could be real in hopes it will stop me from crying when I think of what you have turned into. Or better yet, what we have turned you into.

Sometimes I wish I could pry my soul away from my flesh and for a day let you be me. Let you be free from all the name calling and hypocrites that pose as your friends and family, but are nothing more than empty shells of who they use to be. I pray when you look at me you will one day find yourself somewhere hidden behind fake memories and useless wishes that I can't seem to let go of, but until then I am sorry. I am sorry that I let you slip into that raging sea of lies and deceit as I sat there afraid that if I tried to jump in to save you I too may be lost. And I know I say this in vain. That my words may never be powerful enough to make you feel my empathy, but I will still scream them to the heavens so that maybe one day when you awaken from your slumber you will hear my words and know I never gave up, but until then I'm sorry. I truly am.

The Poem that will never be

I called you my hero, so I guess that makes me your fool.

I thought I gave you my all, but my heart was still beating and you wanted that too.

You didn't want it to keep it safe, but to throw me into an inevitable future of broken smiles and crushed dreams.

You left me alone singing cries of despair, trying to figure out where I went wrong.

There was nothing left for me but shattered pieces of a foolish heart, waiting to be turned to ash by the suns mocking smile.

It was over.

It was done.

I guess it was never meant to be.

A Talk in the Mirror

I want a change
I want to be free
Let my words be heard
Let my people be

O be quiet you fool
For you know not the facts
You are nothing more than stupid
So shut up and pretend you know how to act

But why should I bite
My tongue till it bleeds
When my heart is telling me
This torment just should not be

It's safer that way
It's best to just blend in
Too much attention
Can be bad in the end

Is that what you want
For your children to be scared
To let them cower
To hide in fear

They should know their place
As you should know yours
Let's not be stupid
Now go and do your chores

Would you see your mom into slavery
While she is screaming out your name

Would you turn your back on your brother
Because you think his cause is in vain

        They knew of the consequences
          Grown they all wanted to be
      That was not my decision but there's,
    So what happens has nothing to do with me

Do you have a heart,
Can you even hear it beat?
What happened to make you so cold?
Who scared you to stay in your seat?

           I saw my father whipped
         And I saw my mother burned
     Sister and brothers got fed to the dogs
        And yet no freedom was earned

I will not ask you
To place yourself in harm's way
But how many more people
Will you let die with your delay

    Can we walk with pride knowing the truth
       Of our ancestors forced to die
     Can we just sit in silence day by day
      Knowing they died for us to survive
         So today I will say
        Let my people be free
         So that years to come
        They will be able to say
    Thank you for paving the way for me

Dream Worlds

We accept the love we think we deserve, so close your eyes and count to 3, maybe then you will dream about me.

We would dance for what seemed like forever and a day. You would hold me, and kiss me, and I swore never to go away. But when the light crept slowly in, I was forced to say goodbye. Our shadows fled, two lovers gone and me just wondering why.

Why did you seem so real?

Your touch, your kiss, our love, this dream made my heart grow still.

I walk around the land of the living, although most are dead. Quietly waiting for night to invade and bring me to freedom inside my head. I let the night drag me in, engulfing me full force. While others scream and cry for the light, I ride to you on the midnight horse.

I search and wait for you to appear, while hour by hour haunted by fear. Whispers of doubt, cries of lies, yet I still wait for my well needed surprise. But as the night fades the lights invade. They call my name like sirens upon the rocky sea, but I can't hide for their calls are dragging me to their reality.

And like that, I'm back to the land of the living, but the night has yet to vanish and still feels like giving.

Your hands intertwine with mine and you say I'm here.
Your touch, your kiss, our love, this dream seems so real.
You smile and say we accept the love we think we deserve
so close your eyes and count to 3, maybe then you'll
dream about me. As the sun sets I say goodbye, for soon
night will capture me and I will come alive.

They eye of a storm

What is to be,
when your trapped in the eye of a storm
trying to get free
and see life in its true form.

You want to see what they see,
and feel what they feel.
Those things that will always flee,
unlike you, out of their free will.

But be careful what you wish,
for occasionally it will come true.
Be mindful when they do,
for you may get lost and lose your way through.

But standing on the outside
looking in at yourself,
holding friends hands, with fingers untied,
can surely be your greatest wealth.

But the change will not come easy,
trying to adjust to the new.
It will without a doubt bring you misery,
but never lose the true you.

Now we sit on the dusty road
as our storm rolls by,
carrying away our heavy load
as we silently say good bye.

Let's talk before the end....

I decided to talk about the last poem before the poem because the last poem is a bit complicated. The last poem is called *Jack and Jill*. This poem is written as a testimony to a friend of mine, but also talks about a hard time when the both of us hit rock bottom. He hit bottom and tried to commit suicide. I hit the bottom and wanted to stop school. Little did we know we were not hitting the bottom, but we were hitting God.

In respect of my friend I won't tell the entirety of his story, but between our two stories there were attempted suicides, deaths, births, relationship drama, family members getting sick, financial struggles, grief, depression, school, family, work and the list just continued. During this particular summer we both fell and didn't want to get back up. It truly felt like nothing we were doing would ever pay off and there was no reason to try anymore. However, while we sat on the ground looking at one another, we realized that we didn't want the other to suffer anymore. We helped pick each other up, and next thing we knew, we were both on our feet.

The poem is confusing, hard to follow and can leave the reader confused, even I get confused reading it at times, but that is how I like it. I chose not to edit this last poem and present it as is because that time period *was* confusing and chaotic for the both of us. We were lost and frustrated. In time though, we finally understood the game. Although we were still losing, we knew how the game was being played and knowing is always half the battle. Today my friend and I are doing just fine. Yes, we have our rough days but who doesn't. With each day we strap on the whole armor of God and face our wolves in the eye. Yea it's scary and yea sometimes one of us falls. It took me a while to learn this lesson, but I know now that when you hit the bottom, there is no place left to go but up, and I'm surely climbing, reaching for the top.

<u>Jack and Jill</u>

Jack and Jill went up the hill to fetch a pail of water.
Jack fell down and broke his crown, and Jill came
tumbling after.

If you are Jack then I must be your Jill, as we clutch hands
starring down the barrel of this gun. I wonder if red riding
hood felt this way staring into the face of the mighty
Lupus. The mighty wolf. We stare into the eager, hungry,
cold eyes of our wolf, who's ready to pull the trigger on
our life. Beneath him the street. Streets outlined with chalk
drawings of dreams that have passed away. Bones of
forgotten wishes, and freshly killed corpses smothered in a
blanket of hatred, dripping off their bodies like a stream of
blood. It stands upon its mountain of destruction, barring
its teeth, smiling. But that was us once, two soldiers apart
of the pack, fighting a war we didn't even know existed.
We took aim, fired, one after the other, raking them up.
Until we looked down and saw the mountain of prayers
and dreams we were standing on. Our prayers and dreams
we shot down, using them as targets, taking aim, firing,
one after the other, raking them up. For the wolf. For the
pack. We rose higher and higher, crushing our dreams,
hoping in the path of our destruction we save the pack.
Find our pail of water, our salvation, a crown. A crown.
Our footprint on the world, a token. We wanted a memory,
a legacy, to save the lives of those who have forgotten how
to dream, not realizing we were becoming the very thing

we wanted to save. You fell. Down, down, down and I watched. If you are my Jack and I am your Jill then I should take this leap too, falling down, down, down. We fell. Clutching hands. Starring down the barrel of this gun. The wolf, a shadow of our past, a ghost ready to pull the trigger on our life.

Boom!
Boom!
Boom!
Another casualty, perhaps, another chance.

For you know Jack and Jill went up the hill to fetch a pail of water. Jack fell down and broke his crown, and Jill came tumbling after. And I'm here with you, because once we hit bottom there's no place left for us to go but up.